"One of the strongest new books I've read in the las[...] *Appetite* by Jon Davis."
--Robert Hass, *Poet*

"Davis's fierce questioning gives *Scrimmage of Appetite* an intellectual and moral urgency that is lacking in much recent American poetry. His poetic stance is closer to that of witness-poets such as Zbigniew Herbert and Czeslaw Milosz, whose work merges the lyric impulse into a disciplined examination of European history."
--Brian Johnson, *The Prose Poem*

"Jon Davis, in the most remarkable weave of lyric and meditations I've read in a long time, catches life in a world driven by appetite, with such authentic watchfulness and richness of memory, that we know at once we are part of his story. . . . I treasure this book. I keep it next to me. I read it over and over. Davis says, Look around you. People decide every morning to live. How do we manage that? These poems are a necessary answer."
--Shirley Kaufman, *Field*

"These [are] frightening, sometimes terrifying, strangely beautiful poems. . . . Davis's poems so deeply probe the human condition that we find ourselves lost in new, perplexing, and unidentifiable territories, where our minds and our preconceived ideas about loss and remembrance, pain and epiphany are completely affected and changed."
--June Owens, *Manoa*

"Davis is as good as DeLillo at playing off our internal hunger for meaning against surface senselessness. And Davis catches this surface brilliantly. No wonder that he seems to like bats (his 'In the Sleep of Reason' is the best poem about bats, and one of the best about an animal, that I've ever read), which not only literally play it by ear, but also like to veer to catch what is quick, as these poems do."
--William Greenway, *American Book Review*

"Davis's fantastic exploration of reality, consciousness, and culture is not to be missed; while its scope and philosophy often emerge parallel to such great poets as Rilke and Whitman, its voice remains among the sharpest and most unique in contemporary poetry."
--Carson Utz, *The Independent*

"These works present linguistic exploration, exciting investigations of reality beyond the localized 'I,' and revelations full of beauty and wit."
--Brenda Hillman, recommendation for Borders' National Poetry Month Selection

"Jon Davis's pieces in this anthology [*The Best of the Prose Poem*] are so off-the-charts terrific that the reviewer has gone out and bought the one Jon Davis book mentioned in his bio-note and [has] . . . advertised it in this magazine, at reviewer's own expense—that's how good this guy is."
--David Foster Wallace, *Rain Taxi*

Scrimmage
of Appetite

Jon Davis

The University of Akron Press
Akron, Ohio

ACKNOWLEDGMENTS

Acting on Tradition: The Institute of American Indian Arts Faculty Show (catalog): "The Woman"; *After Five and On Weekends: The Institute of American Indian Arts Faculty Show* (catalog): "In History"; *American Letters & Commentary:* "American Night" and "Contingency"; *ArtSpirit:* "A Broth" and "Island Life"; *Cape Discovery: The Fine Arts Work Center Anthology:* "The Hawk. The Road. The Sunlight After Clouds"; *Five Fingers Review:* "The Year 2000," "The Levelled Site of the Page," "A Sheen, A Radiance," "The Eye of Delight," and "A Closet Full of Excruciations"; *Gulf Coast:* "Marriage"; *Hambone:* "Memory" and "Solo"; *The Harvard Review:* "The Sorry Part"; *Manoa:* "The Ritualized Forms," "A Letter to the Future," and "Gold Card"; *Nimrod: International Journal of Prose & Poetry:* "Before the Rains," "Damage," and "A Desperate Longing for Presence"; *Ontario Review:* "The Story of My Life by Angela Winona Smith"; *The Prose Poem: An International Journal:* "The Frogs," "The Bait," "In History," "Blues," "Relativity," "The Signature," "Meanwhile," "The Common Man," "An American," and "Inside"; *Provincetown Arts:* "Café"; *Quarterly West:* "Gone" and "The Wheel of Appetite"; *Shankpainter:* "Relativity"; *Sonora Review:* "A Party of Sorts"; *yefief:* "Oblivion's Mouth," "In the Sleep of Reason," and "In Privacy."

A number of these poems appeared in a chapbook, *The Hawk. The Road. The Sunlight After Clouds.* (Owl Creek Press, 1995). Several poems were shown in the Sena West Gallery and in the Institute of American Indian Arts Museum.

Thanks, also, to the National Endowment for the Arts, The Fine Arts Work Center in Provincetown, The Maryland State Arts Council, The Massachusetts Council on the Arts and Humanities, The General Electric Foundation and the Coordinating Council for Literary Magazines, and Peter I. B. Lavan and the Academy of American Poets for grants, fellowships, and awards which enabled me to complete this book.

Finally, thanks to my wife, Terry, and daughter, Grayce, for their support and their stories, to Jerome Bruner for his writings, and to Fred Vandenheede, Shirley Kaufman, Dick Allen, Patricia Goedicke, Elton Glaser, and, especially, Greg Glazner and Arthur Sze, for close reading and suggestions.

All inquiries and permissions requests should be addressed to the Publisher, The University of Akron Press, 374B Bierce Library, Akron, Ohio 44325-1703.

LIBRARY OF CONGRESS CATALOGING IN PUBLICATION DATA

Davis, Jon, 1952–
    Scrimmage of appetite / Jon Davis.
        p.   cm. — (Akron series in poetry)
    ISBN 1-884836-11-9 (alk. paper) — ISBN 1-884836-12-7 (pbk.: alk. paper)
    I. Title.   II. Series.
PS3554.A934912S37   1995
811'.54—dc20   95-24381
                                                                    CIP

Manufactured in the United States of America

FIRST EDITION

Contents

III. The Ochre World: A Sequence

for Teresa

for Grayce

for Gregory, Briana, & Matthew

Amid the hundred million of his kind,
The scrimmage of appetite everywhere.

—Delmore Schwartz,
"The Heavy Bear Who Goes With Me"

1. Tumult

You go from dream to dream inside me. You have passage to my last shabby corner, and there, among the debris, you've found life. I'm no longer sure which of all the words, images, dreams, or ghosts are "yours" and which are "mine." It's past sorting out.

—Thomas Pynchon, *Gravity's Rainbow*

Days of Forgetting

These are the days of forgetting, of sensation and synapse.

When, in the cartoon, the video creatures leaped from the
screen and began wandering through the rooms of
the house, the artist, the writer, the machinery of the
discursive formation stumbled onto a truth.

Instructions: Shake it and it begins snowing.

"Wherever you find yourself," someone, perhaps in the
mid-sixties, once said, "there you are."

The world is "whatever is the case."

Whatever is the case, where "whatever" is a loping crane,
where "the case" is a construction worker's
inappropriate, but, to some, flattering scrutiny.

Staple your heart to a paper flower and fold once.

Hit the space bar until the corn begins rustling in the breeze.

When the tourists discovered, at Chaco Canyon, that they
had stepped over a rattlesnake on the trail up, they
returned to taunt it with a stick and a camcorder.

The tiny man, bare to the waist, kept kicking and flipping
even when his handlers left the room.

"That's how I want to be," said one of the boys, making
himself stiff as a machine, spinning and kicking at the
family dog.

Memory

The radio is playing John Lennon's "Imagine" and I have to stand and walk around the room because walking is a defense against feeling, the past, memory. Is a way of swimming when the past washes over and tries to fill the lungs. But there is no defense against memory.

I remember walking in Provincetown, the air thinned by an approaching storm, how the sand and gravel underfoot sounded poignant, and how to explain that? The harbor kept its surf and sadness to itself. The highway was a secret only the eye could unfold.

Listen: I mean to tell you for no good reason how it felt to walk that night alone going on lonely, considering physics: how sound moves through air, the way a rock's vibrations move through water, whether these sounds my feet kept making were stronger than the same sounds on a clear day and what other differences. I was thinking about timbre, how a sort of hollowness—foghorn at night, merest rustlings of a dry oak leaf, a woman's footsteps on the stairs—could stir my body or bring me near tears.

It's not the brain or the mind or something the ear knows how to do. It's not the body making its own rules. It's not memory alone or the present with its fistful of facts, but the way memory reaches out with its little arms and weary voice: "Don't leave me here. I have been waiting for someone to get me out of this house, walk me to the bus stop, ride with me though there is nowhere to go."

I'm speaking of hollowness, the richness of something with something missing—dry riverbed, abandoned nest, the promise that is not a promise, scrape of boot against sand in the lee of a storm. Because memory is a hollow in the body. Because memory is an animal, a sad, furry thing curled in that hollow.

I am thinking of that family in Brazil who found a radioactive canister and took it home because they'd been waiting for it forever and didn't know it. Who placed it on the table and watched. Because it was beautiful and seemed a gift from the gods. Because now, finally, they had it.

I know what you're thinking: That canister is a metaphor for nothing. People were maimed and killed and it was real. Forgive me. I am placing this canister on the table. It is memory and throws a terrible light. Now the body will pour out all of its beauty and grace. Now, unable to bear it, I will stand and walk around this room.

What Passeth for a God

While the herbal tea steeped, idealists boarded the subway,
incendiary devices in their laps.

A husband and wife inventing the modern constellations:
Dog-At-The-Door, Car-Broken-Down, Stratocaster,
Meaningless Blob, Elvis's Hair.

Not the life of the mind. Not *that.*

What he wanted from her was incommensurate with his
politics.

She leaned over him, letting her breasts fall against his face.

His gratitude was a text they could not completely decipher.

Dear M., he wrote, years later, *when this anger is finally*
absorbed in the abstract quality that blurs our motives, call
me, and we'll live busily ever after.

They are, it's true, seated at the right hand of what passeth
for a god.

In the myth, Coyote swallows Hummingbird and becomes
human.

But what about us? she asked when the story was over. *What*
about us?

The silence swarmed about them like bees.

No motive for the firebomb is known, the cheerful announcer
said, *but investigations are ongoing.*

Coyote, realizing—in one shuddering instant—what
Hummingbird had always known, began howling and
slapping his pockets, feeling for his wallet.

The Turtle: An Eccentric Ode

What if the past is inescapable? Summer, and the quicksilver tunes from America's last aerials—mockingbirds singing robin, thrush, mew of a cat, pool filter rattle. In those days, the men were obsessed with business and loss. The women dabbed their moist foreheads with damp sleeves. The paperbacks were splayed, spines broken, on the concrete walkway around the pool.

North of town, where we lived, the trains hooted and hooted. When I was a child when I was a child. I lived in a straw hut outside the village. In a hole in the ground. In a cave. Which explains everything: the trembling when I speak, the long silences at the sink washing and washing my hands, the guitar solos I welcome into my house.

What if the past is inescapable—the father lifting the knife into the bulblight to threaten the mother, the shotguns loaded and aimed, the mother stiffening and buckling under the shocks; then, one day, a family seemed possible—the rafts blown up, flippers and masks, a latticed porch, a few waves, sand, then the air pressed out and home again to a house full of strangers.

Years later, the misfits I called my friends would leap in front of trucks, hang themselves, drink too much and fast, let guilt glue its electrodes to their heads. The few who survived say *It's a living it's a living what did we expect?* When I was a child when I was a child.

One day a spotted turtle turned-up by my grandmother's cane in the brook beside the house. One day a silver dollar-sized turtle in a puddle no bigger than the galvanized tub my dying grandfather soaked his feet in. To the turtle, the puddle must have seemed like an ocean. To me, the marvel was one of scale—how small the turtle and puddle, how shallow and yet sufficient.

What if the past is inescapable? Forget, for now, the part about the fishbowl, the carnivorous diving beetles, the turtle's severed head, the hank of neck skin fluttering in the churned-up water. Think instead of the living turtle, the soft, churning, yellow-striped legs, the needle-like claws, the slick black shell, the red brush strokes fringing the carapace, the smooth head, the tiny striped eyes, blinking, the feel of the whole cool turtle nudging and prying at my own soft, cupped, six-year-old hands.

Marriage

In Chagall's *Birthday*, the man floating nearly off the canvas
   twists his neck impossibly to complete the shape
   suggested by the woman's face.
She holds a bouquet lightly in her hand.
The rest of the scene is domestic: A butter knife, two plates,
   a coin purse; behind them, a bed, tapestries, perhaps a
   mirror.
But she is leaving the room. That is the first secret of the
   painting.
Though she appears to walk on the red floor, she is already
   tilted impossibly forward.
He snakes above her like smoke or mist drawn along by the
   gravity of her leaving.
She drifts toward the window, toward the angular repetitions
   of the dawn that is just beginning outside.
Or maybe it's a well-lit night. This is 1923, and lights are
   coming on all around the world.
But that's not the point.
His eyes are closed, his arms, hidden, useless.
She's pushing off lightly with the toe of her right foot.
He has closed his eyes to kiss her.
Her eyes are wide, her gaze drawn to the lights dazzling the
   gray sky.
She has already relinquished the flowers.
The painting is called *Birthday*, and they are drifting like
   balloons toward the future.
In a moment he will bump the window sash, crumple to the
   floor, and awake.
She will slip through the crack and be gone.
And that is the other secret of the painting and why Chagall
   stopped them with his art.

He will never fall now.
She will never drift off.
The painting concerns marriage.
That is why, love, I woke early and wrote this while you slept.

Fish Magic

after Klee

In another painting, death wants its skeletons revealed.

Here, surfaces wear their blue desires. An ocean of air. Daisy
    in the sky. In water? A fish. A clock. The moon.

According to the once-longed-for apocalypse, this should be
    fire, should be ice.

According to The Map of the History of the World, land is
    ocean, then ocean land.

So this woman/man, this two-faced diver leaning to these
    flowers?

She stands knee-deep in art; he's mired in imagination.

The whole sky floats above them: fish wearing their pink
    ideas, the face in which nine o'clock lives, daisy with its
    scale-like leaves.

A moon.

Two moons.

One moon like a void in memory; the other like a fish's eye.

Red longs to enter the canvas.

Red presses up against the darkness like a cat against a screen.

Like a woman's breasts against lace.

In the bluest corner, a man in a dunce cap is filled with ideas.

Is trying to see.

Stars coming out.

The clock encased in glass and two pieces of fruit keeping
    time afloat.

The dunce in the bluest corner has only a white feeling about
    time.

Two eyes, if you could call them that.

A nose.

A spattering of freckles.

Like stars, leaning into the scene.

The Bait

This is not an elegy because the world is full of elegies and I am tired of consoling and being consoled. Because consolation is unsatisfying and even tenderness can do nothing to stop this loss, this dying, this viciousness among men.

And god just complicates, offering justice like the cracker I place on this mouse trap. Then frantic mouse hands pushing against the metal bar, kicking and bucking, the fall from the shelf, more kicking, one eye bulging, lips lifted and the little yellowed teeth clamped on the small crumb of goodness that was not goodness but something alluring and, finally, dumb—without equivalent in the human world. Just food he couldn't have.

My food and what that means in the scale of human affairs. I didn't want to listen to this mouse scrabbling among the graham crackers, chewing into the can of grease, leaving a trail of greasy, orange, rice-like shits in the cabinet under the sink. I didn't want to clean those up every morning; I didn't want to be awakened in the night.

I set the trap; the trap smashed his skull; he kicked awhile and he died. I tossed him, trap and all, into the dunes. But I was saying something about god and justice. I was saying this is not an elegy and why. Because pain is the skin we wear? Because joy is that skin also?

Because . . . look: I had a brother and he died. I didn't cause it; I couldn't stop it. He got on his motorcycle and rode away. A car turned in front of him and that began his dying. How terrible for everyone involved. Do I sound bitter? I felt the usual guilts: Did I love him enough. Did I show it.

It happened eleven years ago and what I remember: Looking out at the lawn, September and a breeze; watching him ride—

flash of red gas tank, brown leather jacket; the sound of the bike; what we said, which I recall as a kind of gesture, the sound of *what are you doing*, some dull rhythm and *see you later.*

The phone call. The drive to the hospital. I think I drove but I can't be sure. We drove the wrong way down a one-way street and I remember feeling responsible. I cried most of the time. I knew he was dying. My brother's girlfriend asked me *Why are you crying?* and I couldn't say or else I sobbed *It's bad I know it's bad.*

Then we were taken into a green room and told he was dead. I curled on a red plastic chair. My body disappeared or seemed to. I was looking for my brother; a nurse called me back: *Your family needs you.* I came back.

But why am I telling you this? Because I want you to love me? To pity me? To understand I've suffered and that excuses my deficiencies? To see how loss is loss and no elegy, no quiet talk late at night among loved ones who suddenly feel the inadequacy of their love and the expression of that love can take it away? Or give it back? Perhaps even loss is lost?

My brother is gone and the world, you, me, are not better for it. There was no goodness in his death. And there is none in this poem, eleven years later and still confused. An attempt, one might say, to come to terms with his death as if there were somewhere to come to, as if there were terms. But there is nowhere to come to; there are no terms. Just this spewing of words, this gesture neither therapy nor catharsis nor hopelessness nor consolation. Not elegy but a small crumb. An offering.

Tumult: Second State

At first, all these parallel lines feeling their way along the crust
 of events.
Like a network of rhizomes.
Like a squadron of wriggling spermatozoa.
What little color there was kept slipping from its assigned
 place; when heads turned, mouths formed their *O*'s on
 the air.
When finches scattered—too many wings.
Then a darkness soaked into the details.
Spread.
At the far end, where circumstance etched its first tentative
 sentence, a woman stepped from a car, throbbing with a
 cantillated music.
In each segment of the emptiness, a bare bulb hung, flared
 briefly, and died.
Geometry failed at every corner.
Conclusions hunkered in a thicket of brushwork, wriggled
 and kicked.
In the drypoint that longed to become grass, a small wren
 flicked its rufous tail and tried to speak.
In the tumult of irradiated lies that kept arranging themselves
 into a semblance of narrative, certain facts buzzed against
 the screen.
The night was hot, humid.
1975, nearly Connecticut, and the couple had already been
 drawn onto the roof.
The streetlight flickered through the maples' fluttering gauze.
A breeze and the impassioned wails of a screech owl.
The future in its well-lit kitchen.
A child, one ear to the register, hearing all the scraps of voice
 trapped and murmuring in the labyrinth of breath.

Café

In what passes for a café in New Haven, Connecticut, he kept telling me things I didn't want to hear. How he wanted to remain in their room and fuck again and again until nothing remained of desire. Then he would know if there was something left to call love. Then an enormous tenderness would light them from within. Or not.

Which is what stopped him. He could not imagine himself, his life, without the fountain of their history to buoy him up. Then he spoke of that character in the Pynchon novel who tells his lover, "We're both being someone new now, someone incredible." The mystical wonder of that. The trick of language.

But this, my friend said, is what scared him most: That he would be the same person forever, make the same mistakes in whatever life he chose, wake to the same miseries—a boxful of unfinished stories, two children whose beauty he was in charge of damaging, a house that would never rest (no honeyed hardwood, oriental rugs, no Mozart dreaming itself into the flower-brightened air).

We tinkered with our spoons in the glass cups while the brass machine hissed and sputtered. "I don't know," he said. "Did you ever feel like this?" The cups seemed ridiculously dainty and fragile. Through the steam-glazed window the street looked like a scene envisioned by Toulouse-Lautrec but executed by Monet. We watched people passing through the streetlight's haze to enter the all-night bookstore across the street. Out of what murky depths they kept coming to be touched so briefly by such blurred, inadequate light.

The Sound

The sound of a hammer mollifies the dawn. The sound
of a hammer malleable in cold air. The sound of a hammer
is a raven folding its wings falling into the valley meadow.
Falling,
as a thought will fall into its opposite. As fingers will suddenly
manifest an intuition.
The sound of a hammer striking a six-penny,
the sound of metal on lesser metal amplified through wood.
A raven
falling. A thought (a remembrance) bursts into a silent room
where the repose of flowers on a wicker table aligns the clutter
of papers and books. A room, where his wife waits—a
wilderness
of feelings, calm privacy, thoughts of the moon and food,
impenetrable demeanors. A raven, falling, like a thought.
Who can unravel this entanglement? Hammer, raven,
flowers, wife.
In "Eastern" music (an impossible designation),
in India (where "India" arises out of the land), the young
musician
sings and plays *Sa* until he carries the note inside him:

shrine   small flame   presence   home.

The Frogs

Fourth of July and the children have grown miserable from turning and turning their wobbly cartwheels, from jump-kicking the forces of evil that throng about us, from dumping Kool Aid on the younger children to attract our flagging attentions. These children who are open to beauty and joy—"Look, Dad! A moth!"—but who quickly weary of the world's surprises as we weary, the parents of all this joy, who wear our silly striped ties—the badges of our race, the honors; who bang our heads against the daily task; who flop on our chaise lounges and rattle the ice in our drinks; who bolt from our homes at mid-life, then return to hammer back the boards through which we burst and live out our lives, pails under all the leaks. Who then fill the wagon with children and drive to a mountaintop to watch meteorites, stars dying across the sky so beautifully we rattle the ice in our drinks and remember the monastery we passed on the drive up, those poor monks who have no cluttered lives against which to measure such purity.

And today we sneak four cars to the frog pond, 17th hole, Manchester Country Club, where we tie monofilament to fishing poles, squares of red flannel to monofilament, and dangle those squares before the appetite of frogs. They turn to face them, mistaking them for butterflies or moths. They leap and wrap their sticky tongues around the flannel, and we, shouting and whooping, fling them onto the fairway, where they flop and sprawl, where we chase them, where they extricate their tongues and hop, stunned, in whatever direction they face. Poor frogs. Poor frogs. Poor deluded creatures.

Island Life

She sang beyond the commerce of the sea.

At two in the morning in the speakeasy dark: the calypso
man, guitar squawking like a parrot in the mangroves.

Jazz in the actual night. Tomorrow: More fruit drinks.

The "iris garden" was actually a field of knives, their handles
planted in the rich loam.

Sense, they all agreed, waiting for the blossoms, is a distant
cousin of meaning.

A pigeon paced like the emperor of nothingness.

Sunlight poured into the courtyard. The limestone walls
pulled wisteria over their cloudy faces.

Any moment, aliens would arrive from the mainland, waving
their paper money, constantly bobbing to the beat of a
single, somnambulant song.

The birds, tired of piercing lizards on the orange trees' spines,
began sucking the oranges dry.

When the wind blew, the empty fruits rustled.

Where the residents saw a threat, the visitors saw a richness.
Approaching, an expert would later write, the symbolic
density of art.

Blues

Forms seek subjects.
—Frank Bidart

The first line must be about heartbreak: "Oh, she stomped my heart / give me the stompin' blues." The second must be the first sung with increasing rage and despair: "Yeah, she STOMPED my heart / gi' me the STOMPIN' blues." The third must add detail and complete the breakage: "She stomped it with my best friend / wore my favorite shoes."

At this point, the guitar may complain or cry. At this point, the singer may moan, "Oh, baby." At this point, a white boy, a construction laborer in work boots and flannel shirt may, having been overcome by the poignancy of the occasion and several draught beers, begin to sway and shout "Amen!" thrusting his plastic cup into the air.

Which may or may not signal the coming of an avant-garde. Say the next time he shouts, "Radiator!" Say the next time he shouts, "Come unto the Lord." Say the next time he shouts, "I'm on fire" or "Stuff the turkey. The kids are in the car and I can't stay long." Say he talks over the bridge, saying, "The cake flopped. The cake flopped. We gave it to the cousin who eats such things."

Say he begins rocking vigorously and continues: "The linoleum's cracking by the fridge. When the welfare lady comes be neat, be clean, but don't be happy. Tell her we never have enough. Tell her we behave anyway. After dark, if we lean the brick palette against the back wall and climb it like a ladder and pull ourselves onto the back porch where the door is always open, we can go inside."

At this point, the guitarist may attack a single note and hold it. "We'll bring a flashlight—a small one—and we'll eat ice cream and cheese and steal the records—Love, Steppenwolf, *The Soft Parade, Dr. Byrd and Mr. Hyde.* When I call your brand of cigarettes, the brand you're thinking of, you run around the yard and I'll try to catch you. Darkness. Toads along the porch. Katydids creaking. Bats. One night we shined a flashlight into the maple and watched small animals hurl themselves onto the roof of the house. Flying squirrels."

He might also mention the way those bats flew—the veering, the way they swooped at the stones he tossed. The stones he gathered from the driveway where the Dugan man parked his bread truck. It would be nearly dark, and he'd climb in the open door with his brothers and eat cherry pies while the Dugan man drank coffee with his grandmother. Then they'd slip out the side door and the bats would be veering above.

Attraction and avoidance. This is the blues. It keeps repeating itself. Keeps repeating its lonesome self. The object is purgation. Catharsis. The object is triumph. Endurance. Humor. At this point, the singer may shout, "Hurt me!" And the guitar may answer, *Pain, pain, pain. Pain, pain, pain.*

"Mystery Blend"

The town worries a hole in the overcast, withering the already stunted corn.

The milky lights along the Rio Grande, under the sunset's roof, cause a man to think of his childhood and, after sitting twenty minutes, turn the key in the ignition and drive slowly home.

Of the many forms that silence takes, the most memorable is the dry husk of the cicada.

The painter, faced with a wall of coffees, chose "Mystery Blend."

Constriction of the blood flow in some artists produces hallucinations which serve as a useful substitute for the imagination.

The imagination, otherwise, is a waltz with nothingness. A series of untestable propositions.

Nothing the president says can alter the molecular structure of a pear.

The addition or deletion of two commas can often determine who is sane, who is insane.

The president, for example, who wanders through the Rose Garden, fascinated by the green-gold beetles which fly so poorly they keep bouncing off his polo shirt.

The clank of horseshoes; secret servicemen standing alertly among the yews.

When my daughter watched the video of herself, she said, "What's that she's holding in my hand?"

Solo

When the guitarist took his solo, it was poorly phrased and off-key and therefore beautiful. And new. Calling into question all that had come before. Calling into question even the question. That there should be questions. That the questions should take this form.

Maybe it was the alcohol or the facts of smoke and noise (the wind of vehicles, the air compacted and hurled out from their passing), the bartenders calling out over the clink and rush of their doing, their *occupation*, we say, as if the task had filled them, had, in fact, *possessed* them, as if what were calling out was this *doing*, not the bartenders themselves, what they had been before.

There was a song, a key, a home, and now it was gone. That the guitarist could live there so briefly and with such confidence. That we could join him in the beautiful error that occupied him. But there were chords to play, a beat to sustain. A bass line against which our transcendence was measured.

Measured, as a man will measure his distance from a flame. A *flame*, by which I mean something dangerous, and sustaining. Something that lives briefly, dies, and therefore houses our needs. Is a metaphor for desire, the metaphor we have chosen for desire. What we call *desire*, a word that pierces the walls of any home we find for it, and thus we have chosen flame for its home.

Which is not what I mean. What I mean is this: I was in a club in Santa Fe with my wife and my best friend and my best friend's wife. This was some years ago, and I did not know what I wanted then as I do not now. But I wanted, we all wanted, and it was our wanting that kept us alive, that brought us to that place. And then the guitarist broke free from the band, their mindless comping, into something beautiful and terrifying. And then he was back.

But why do I make up these stories? That guitarist was on the radio, yesterday, and—though it reminded me of the feeling I had in that club in Santa Fe—he wasn't there that night. But I hadn't intended to lie. I began with that guitarist which led to some amateur philosophical speculation, which led to what?

Something happening in my actual heart, or between my heart and my stomach, what the medical books call a *thrill*. Which felt like loneliness, the way loneliness feels when it surprises you—my wife and daughter were away for the weekend and I have not seen my friend and his wife since that night in the club.

But I wanted to make something beautiful. I wanted our lives to have the grace of that solo. Though it was wrong. Though it was brief and embarrassed the other band members. Though even the guitarist, when he was finished, seemed not to know what he'd done. Or so I imagine, since I didn't actually see him.

I wanted our lives to have the grace of that solo. And I love the guitar, how its voice comes from the hands and not the lungs. How our intentions so easily go awry or how our actual intentions are made clear. But the guitarist in Santa Fe was controlled and accurate and so of little interest.

I remember the table and our drinks, the limes and swizzle sticks, the circles we made with our glasses on the wet Formica. We must have talked about the music. It was an open mike night and so invited judgment.

What I remember most were the failures of a young saxophonist who'd come over from the high school to sit in, how his solos were built on five notes, five notes that were absolutely right and so offered no hope. That's what I remember. And going back outside.

Stars, lights, the stylish bustle of a Santa Fe night. We didn't quite know where the car was or if there was a car. We were looking in the windows of shops, crossing the narrow streets, weaving a little and laughing. Maybe it had cooled off and we were shivering. Above us, a breeze gathered itself in the cottonwoods—brushes and bass, piano sketching a chord, the first tentative gestures of a tenor sax.

A Story

And this is when he took you—
the four of you—into the woods
in a black Ford? I like the sound
of "black Ford," the drama.
"Black Ford" makes the car gleam,
makes it beautifully sinister.
But he took you—the four of you—
into the woods? He'd called
your mother and threatened
to steal you and then he did?
Branches brushed
against the windows of the car.
Pale green, those branches,
and dust motes circulating in sunlight.
I've written this down before.
Then the black and silver of cops.
And where was your mother? Home,
"wringing her hands," as we say
when we speak of mothers, the fifties.
But, surely? She "wasn't well."
Maybe she just watched
as he drove away. Maybe she
"hurried onto the porch." Maybe
she trusted him. You hear such stories
all the time: a man, a woman;
she gives him "one more chance."
Why must you keep telling
this particular story?
It seems to explain some things.
"Things"? When we arrived
at the police station, we, no,

I was confused. It was,
after all, my father
with the handcuffs on.
There was damage being done
and there was candy—a machine
with a mirror. I was torn.
The officer bought us candy.
The handcuffs made my father
lean forward. He seemed never
to straighten up after that.
You like this part of the story?
It was nice being kidnapped.
I didn't know about the killing part
until later. *Why do you always*
tell about the candy machine?
It was pretty—the shiny wrappers,
bright colors, the mirror, the worn-
smooth knobs. I was distracted,
but not entirely.
Who do you blame?
I don't remember being happy
when my mother and uncle
came to take us home.
I probably wanted another
candy bar. I've seen this
in children—their parents die
and they want new toys,
a snack. We must have gone
outside to the car—
of course we did—
but I keep seeing the candy

and then, in the margin,
some familiar faces. *So
the theme is the triviality
of tragedy, of family?* No,
the theme must be in the mirror,
in the turning away. *In small pleasure
staving off the big sadness?*
That could be it.
That would be very—
what would you call it?
American? Yes, American,
and afterwards a drive in the country.

II. In History

Winds are coming from the future
with mysteriously beating wings
—Friedrich Nietzsche

You got the sound of the modern loneliness.
—Jonathan Richman & The Modern Lovers

The Sorry Part

This is "the sorry part" and the father is laughing. The girl, who has tormented the boy and the boy's family. The angry, the *single-minded* sister. The too-handsome. The witty. The self-involved. All, in an instant, transformed. Insight already shaping itself into the florid Latinates of confession and forgiveness. The inwardness displayed on the screen, the signs of inwardness, the training grown crucial and apparent, the eyes cast down, the timing, oh, the timing. This is the sorry part and the father is laughing—*who does he think he is?*

For an hour, the family has watched, together, the plot unscrolling. For an hour, minus the numerous other minutes blossoming with products and the pantheon of imagery—flowers, endangered species, muscles, and sweat in this age of lives measured backward from absence.

For an hour, the family has endured the thoughtless, the captive of Beverly Hills, wandering through their inane traumas —kiss, sleep, banish some other from one's life, wash cars, build a float for some parade celebrating banality, phone calls, some Puccini played with mock passion on a small stage, then gasoline poured dramatically on something they were supposed to want preserved, some *property.*

For an hour, and, now, this is the sorry part. The past, suppressed so long, wriggles up like a frog out of the mud, blinking its eyes. The past with its clichéd bellowing. The past with its eloquent soliloquies. The past with its arm in a sling. With its mazes where the lost children keep wandering, creating a kind of gyroscope that assures the orbit of their lives will be erratic, elliptical.

This is the sorry part, the five-year-old says. She knows this part. She has lain in bed and heard how these stories unfold.

First the mother speaks sharply, then the father shouts, then both grow silent. Time passes, during which she sleeps and dreams of dragons and ducks.

Then the long, earnest conversation which is music with duration and timbre but without melody. Doors slammed at intervals. At intervals, the brass of complaint and amelioration. Then birds singing and a light in the trees. Soon, then, the sorry part.

One must not laugh. The birds are singing. The earth is rolling like a whale in a calm sea, letting the sun wash over its gray flanks. There will be speeches or there will be no speeches. The script is meaningless. This is form and drama. First the man and woman love each other and then the man and woman love each other. In between, they stare at the window expecting darkness but see instead their own watery, ineffable forms.

One must not laugh. One must lie in bed and wait. One must rise seriously and slip down the hall, bare feet on stone—the slapping sounds of bare feet hurrying on stone—to press the bedroom door open, walk in and stand, poised in morning sunlight and the certainties of form.

Gone

In the middle of it a red sign kept blinking: BOWL BOWL
BOWL. On the one hand, commerce had thrown all these
losers over its bony shoulder. On the other, these striped red
shoes for a small rental fee, these balls off the rack that will
never fit these hands, the marvelous, endlessly replaceable lug-
gers and heavers, the vanilla cokes stirred at the counter where
the waitress fancies herself something of a star, are a kind of
choir to attenuated pleasure.

Think of it: The dock workers and carpenters, the hangers
from poles, the twisters of copper, the short-haul truckers in
their shirts that announce "MAMMON CITY MOVING" and
their own smaller scripted names, each satisfied for these hours
to hear the thunk and rumble and clatter of pins, then the ball
skidding out of its dark, brush-lined tunnel to totter and spill
into a circle with the others, clacking softly.

What could be better? Men and women far from the scowling
bosses, the mailmen with their fists full of bills, far from the
modern casualty of undress and its consecutive euphemisms—
another kind of work—who wear their several gloves: this
actual glove that pads the greedy palm, this glove of the not-
quite-loved, this of ever-increasing despair.

Meanwhile, the babysitter has wrestled the kids into the corner
of the couch and is sitting on them until the parents return.
Meanwhile, the babysitter has concocted Odor of Rotten Egg
from the vials of chemicals in the tri-folded metal case.
Meanwhile, the two teenaged daughters have invited two
weaving drug-gulpers into the tent Dad pitched for them in
the rotting orchard. But not now, not now.

Greg is working on five strikes; Joe is looking for a fill. Anne is
drying her hand over the blower, staring into the void between

the 7 and 10 like it's the distance between desire and its object. She's looking for all the world like she's going to make it, this time, for once and for all of us gawking from the welded row of plastic chairs clutching our rags and rosin bags like rosaries. That sure of ourselves. That gone.

The New Americans

They are rising from duckweed shoals on slippery haunches,
   front feet changed into grasping hands, thumbs and
   forearms thickened for commerce, mouths too bony for
   kissing.
They will breathe through their skins.
Their eyes will be keened for motion.
They will be maculate, stricken with appetite.
They will lunge with purpose, long tongues speaking the
   language of capture, shouting the single verb of longing
   in the dialect of hunger.
They will grunt and snore nightly in the tall grass.
While gods, made in their image, bellow beside the river of
   heaven, they will jockey in the weedbanks.
They will turn, nothing human in their eyes, just the hard
   measure—the precision, the unswerving focus.
They will be mystics wired to the gods' wishes.
They will leap before they know they are leaping.

The Year 2000

Often before we built our hopes on a handful of numbers. How we cheered when all the fives came up on the odometer, the cash register receipt. The day took on a momentous aspect: *We'll be lucky in love and finances!* But then the next day came with its jumble of numbers, its facts that wouldn't announce their allegiances.

It's a complicated world and the temporary clarity of three zeroes is enough to make all of us climb onto our high horses. *Self-fulfilling prophecy,* someone says. Spoilsport. Unbeliever in luck and magic. The vaunted will, even laboring in the sweatshop of the heart, keeps its jacket and tie on, its coif stays voluptuous and tidy. It keeps droning about the stock exchange, cold fronts, situation comedies. Recites mileage and routine maintenance as if they were the works of Shakespeare. Strange reverence for the daily chore.

But maybe we all come to that. Or make chores of Shakespeare and Smokey Robinson alike. Even these dance steps have about them an aspect of seriousness I don't remember them having. Shouldn't joy be uncoiling in the body? Doesn't it live in the heart, kicking like a baby with its single appointment? Doesn't it keep reaching up to calm the silly brain? And doesn't the brain keep remembering death and worrying the body with its cries of *slow down, lean hard right, don't put that in your mouth?* While the genitals, those blessed plutocrats, keep paying off the brain? So we live by a kind of corrupt economy, turning to sex the way a dying plant turns its last energies to producing a single flower.

Of course, we can't forget the underlying dialectic: The "special interest groups" applauding themselves, lobbying for attention. That's a metaphor arising from the economic base, the means of exchange, so in a society in which we conceal the true nature of our daily exchanges from ourselves, the internal economy is also mysterious. But, knowing this, can't we throw off the yoke of imperialism? Can't we choose a fiction and live it? Can't we declare a democracy of the body?

We must wait, it seems. We must wait. Down there in front of the Donut Shoppe, beside the yellow sign, in front of the green bench. A crowd has already gathered. They're checking their watches, brushing the lint off their suits. Those few with hats have taken them off and have begun brushing the hair off their foreheads. Some have newspapers, a few wear head-phones. One sits on the bench with a pocket video game. He's saying *doo doo* as he manipulates it, his fingers fluttering over the red and blue buttons. Others look on, feigning disinterest. Like most of us, they're fascinated. Like most of us, they're appalled.

Relativity

In college I took a course in the philosophy of science. The professor, who held a degree in physics, spent half the quarter lecturing about Einstein, Heisenberg, quantum mechanics, going over formulae, drawing little pictures of men on trains, men in rockets, photons striking or not striking or zipping through an imaginary hole in an imaginary plate. For the first time I understood something about physics. For the only time, and I went around campus seeing things in a new light. Pouring coffee into my styrofoam cup seemed an amazing act. Light fell thickly or not thickly on the carpet that kept making itself improbably green. I understood things I have not understood since. Not the old $E=mc^2$, the sort of thing one sees on television game shows where the answer in the form of a question please is "What did Einstein say?" but something deeper, at once more mundane and more magical.

But, of course, it was already out there, in the movies and books, in the solos Charlie Parker played as he backed us into the 20th century we were already in the middle of. In the gold space suits these dancers wear on this TV show and in the flannel shirts my friends wear against the future. In the way this poem can veer from Einstein to the photograph of a Yapese villager wearing a Budweiser can headdress to the newspaper article I have tacked to my wall: "Four Glued Down Before Stickup," in which a man enters Wayne's Bait & Tackle in Osage, Missouri, sticks four people to the floor with an industrial-sized tube of fast-drying glue, and steals an undetermined amount of cash. "John got up first," John's wife told the reporter. "He was glued on the hands and between the eyes. You could see it running down his cheeks. It only took a few minutes to get free. When you're *sacred*," the article said, "you can do anything."

Of course, she meant *scared,* but the typesetter had a hangover or too many cups of coffee, or the proofreader was having trouble with her boyfriend, whom she suspected was "seeing" a friend of a friend, a woman she'd despised since she first watched her place her impeccably manicured hand under her blonde hair and lift it—in a gesture she'd seen too often on television—flirtatiously off her shoulder at a football game in Perryville.

Of course she meant *scared,* but it came out *sacred*, as it does in the Old Testament, or in that little rocket ship travelling at the speed of light, in which the diminutive man grows old watching his tiny wife and tinier children stand on the launch pad, motionless, frozen in the sad yet hopeful postures of farewell, knowing that they have already escaped that prison of light, but unaware that his wife has already remarried, this time to a miniature alcoholic ironworker who beats her and the children until they get big enough to beat him back, that his daughter has gotten pregnant, lost the child, gotten pregnant again, divorced the accountant and married the stockbroker, that his son has lost a leg in a motorcycle accident, collected the insurance money, grown first sullen, then bitter, and drunk himself to death.

But the little man puts his feet up on whatever passes for a hassock in a rocket ship and watches—for the umpteenth time— a movie called *Life & Death,* knowing what his science has taught him: That he rides on the present as a hollow plastic ball will ride a fountain, that he is beyond the reach of shouts and cries, that the past will break over him disguised as the present and he will be helpless to intervene.

American Night

The surge and bash of the wind.

Invent us, whisper the ponderosas, the scarf of mist
being drawn between ridges, being teased into
the darkness between branches, creating
depth while the honky-tonk radio
shouts its betrayal and its four-four time.

Blankness of landscape, will you
call him? Will you make for him a song that
singing, cannot be sung? The red-haired woman,
the woman at the back of memory at the back
of the song, is the answer to the question, but
the question?

Dear Muse: we made a passage through
time, made correspondence and vexation
our subjects. Here is where the pedal
steel. Here is where the Buick. Here
is where the barmaid. Here is where
Wittgenstein objects to the parade
of correspondences—he, she, did such-and-such
and the affixing of blame. (Are they
even awake this late? And why the horns, now,
when so much has already happened?)

On this side of town, they are gathering
a university. On this side,
maybe the stoved-in and transmogrified bodies
of a thousand Buicks. What does your country
song say about that? A woman
has lined up her lipsticks and
her nail polishes and is testing
their effects, but, mostly,

the night is painting
the inside of this box
called "The City." Mostly,
we have forgotten how to tilt the pail, how to wrap the rope
around the hand when we lean over the well and see
our silhouettes there among the stars.

Here is where history enters the melody, shouting and
     sweating among the rows.

Here is where we glimpse the white frame church behind the
     chords.
And the emptiness.
And the emptiness
where the mother. Where
the father shakes the newspaper
straight. Where the man in
rattlesnake boots makes the guitar

makes the guitar rumble then
whine. So you think it's a train,
do you? A train, which is an emblem
for leaving, which is a scene
photographed in black and white
in which all the men wear
felt hats. In which the women
are tearful in the face of,

well,
loneliness. Which is the theme
that enters the soundhole
and can't find its way out.

Meanwhile, an actual train is using
gravity to assault the earth, is using
the air to make a sound which is not
music, exactly, though each engineer
has, it seems, composed a different
diminished tune, a signature of sorts
to announce his arrival to nobody
listening, in the small towns and villages,
in the grid loneliness spreads
over the land. In some

cladograms, the tongue is cousin to the slug.
But hungrier. And hunger is in the song.
This is the part where death puts its thumb out,
the part where the highway is unlit, where the singer
is a darkness leaned against the gleam
of a fender. A beer bottle tilted. This

is where the piano convinces him
that his genetic inheritance, that
the back of his father's hand. This
is where the piano says, *shift gears, drive,*
this is the beautiful ruin
you were made for.

Then the drums pick it up
like a quickening pulse. And the neon
says EAT. And the neon says
GAS. And the signifiers call him out
into the wax and glitter of an American night.

The Sixties: Two Scenes

1. In the Church / 4th of July / Derby, Connecticut

Once the mercury flowed in Danbury and found the river down there. The children kept climbing the hills. Kept sliding back down. Posters, papers, incense. Stoned and adrift on the water bed. Wine in a paper bag. A park full of promise. When they finally sent the police in. Whose children were they? He carried his flute everywhere he went. The door to the church was open. Someone blew every candle out. The light from the parking lot glowed against the stained-glass windows. Flute song like torn wind. Like a flame. Anything could happen. The man on the cross kept opening his arms. The Grand Finale was about to begin. Flute song. Flute song. Detonations through the church walls.

2. Listening

Standing on the lake. Winter. There were more drugs in there, he said. His eyes kept trying to escape his face. Later, he would live with cows in Massachusetts. Would work in a pickle factory. Later he would live in a hole in the ground. All winter, he said, digging deeper when it got cold, sliding the darkness over his head. Here is the sun, dazzling the lake. Surfaces full of presence. Hendrix wanted us all to. Hendrix kept appearing in the form of smoke. The world was frozen over. Later, on an oil rig in Texas, the boom would thump his head and the medical team would suspect a brain lesion. Hendrix, he'd whisper to the spinning record, what do you want from us?

The Story of My Life by Angela Winona Smith

In this story my brother dies, doused with gasoline, torched by crack dealers an arm's length from the window of my apartment near Father Panic. I watch, clutching a statue of Jesus Christ, Our Father of the Sideways Glance, and do not intervene. I stand behind the drapes, and the long story of my addiction unfolds—the nights spent walking the bridge, starved for smack, for the smooth shackle to be clamped round my neck, my veins crying you must die you must die until I nearly jumped, or thought I did, or did jump.

Look, I am poor and black, educated, literate to a degree. I have read in the Greater Bridgeport Community Mental Health Center several of the novels of Stephen King. The one about the dog in the car. The one about the car. But I shed those fears like a whore sheds her clothes. No dog can get down and growl like what has got me by the throat. No car playing songs whose power was used up in the fifties can lock me inside and make me want to die.

My wanting scratches its belly and opens its hundred yellow mouths. My death is parked in my brain. On an oil-black street in Bridgeport, under the lit-up windows of factories and warehouses. The shattered and caged, the dust-clogged windows. Street of bottle-smash and piss-stain, scrap-metal and trash-can-blaze. Street of School-Bus-Painted-Green. Of the loops of orange spray paint and the gray bag of clothes. Of bypass and overpass and underpass, of *Chico the San-Man & Marie*, of *Mad Dog & Big Eater*, of *Fuck* & *Fuck* & *Fuck* & *Kill*. My death—the keys knock against the column.

Deep in my brain, out by the coliseum, by the highway with its wet-looking cars—the Subaru where the rock tries to burst the windows, the Pontiac throttled by Jam Master Jay. My friend Luie says, "Listen to that. They wrote a song about me and left me here." This is a big dog. A stray with its head tucked low between its shoulders. Quiet and deadly as the first touch of a hurricane that blows, warm and damp as your boyfriend's breath, flipping the pages of a sidewalk magazine where the man is forty and loosening his tie, where the woman is ten years old and is doing what she is told.

In History

The room was an emblem for loneliness—no toast in the toaster, blinds carefully parted. One finger, tugging. The neighborhood was full of strangers. He recognized that. They argued in front of, no, behind their picture windows. The bullet would have already entered, piercing the newly reupholstered davenport. No: *couch*. That was the name history had found for it. "Late in the Twentieth Century there was a great spiritual awakening." Announcers on some channels kept saying that. It was a voice-over while the many well-groomed Americans looked skyward. Later, they would play the Super Bowl. Everyone had to watch or be left speechless at break time. The man entered the woman from behind. Later, they would pass a law. He couldn't help feeling that objects were pressing up against his eyes. He tried to push them away. If he could have painted what he saw. If he could have written it down. The crowd was cheering in unison. In unison, they wanted the quarterback dead or maimed.

Outside, a building rose until it filled the window. There were no shots. Not yet. But he couldn't help feeling he had caused them. He had wanted to move the couch. To hang the Monet on the wall above the stereo. He had wanted to obliterate his feelings. Quit his job. Burn the house. He had wanted to place a single rose in a thin, crystal bud vase. He muted the television with the remote. The woman moaned a little; he whimpered, grateful. Opening his eyes, he saw the building, people slapping hands: 49er fans. *Gold rush.* History was incomprehensible. Intolerable. The blinds were barely parted. The bullet already tearing through fabric, the cotton batting splashing around the bullet. An emblem of his sickness. He should kiss her afterward. He should explain himself to the dust motes circulating in the afternoon light. But she was gone. He was listening to the Pentagon spokesman: "Bomb damage assessment is an art, not a science." He wondered about the implication of this confusion. And why did he think of it now? We leave him there, wondering. We resist his attempts to draw us into the puzzle. He leans to touch the already unscarred fabric.

Contingency

*Alas, in such times as now, when we are in the midst of the Age of
Five Deteriorations, many of the great realized beings have passed
away, and this world is filled with people like myself who speak non-
sense.*

—Jamyang Khyentze Rinpoche, *The Opening of The Dharma*

Chickens on the highway. Moon behind a cloud.
Lightning like capillaries in a bloodshot eye.
A train where there is no train. The woman in white
held a lantern when she drifted into the room.
The spirit of the dead man moved, rising
from the bed where he'd killed himself
ten years before. "The nature of truth
is an unprofitable topic," said Richard Rorty
in London on a cool, foggy evening or an afternoon
of brittle sunlight. His voice was thick
with a kind of joy.
                        Once a stranger came
to a whole town of believers and their handsome children.
Everywhere they looked they saw Truth:
coming from England, packed in the books,
rung down from the church bells, drifting
over the courtyard like the fragrance of lilacs.
The names of things held hegemony:
Brahms' waltzes. Shakespeare's sonnets.

A professor the stranger admired but could not agree with
stood with him in the Halls of Truth and worried that
Shakespeare *was perhaps no smarter than us.* Down the hall, his-
tory kept spouting its official lies. Crazy Horse was: a) A noble
savage, b) A crazy Indian, c) An Indian who, because he fought
whites and did it well, came to think and act like a white man,
or d) An eagle who came to live among us in human form. He
had no time for women or sex and was, therefore, a perfect

hero. Like Custer, he loved war and tried to make it an art. Custer and his orchestra mounted on white horses. Custer and his "regal carriage." He would ride miles to save an animal and loved to punish his men. Contingency.

We keep being in history, a source
of endless terror and delight. "All we need,"
said Richard Rorty on a sunny day in history,
February, 1986, "is to create an ever larger
and more variegated ethnos." Not Truth
with its small army of the saved, but the story
that begins *His hand was raised, we thought*
he had a gun and ends *We took him in,*
fed him, learned his language.
He became like a brother, and to think,
one day we wanted to kill him.

A larger and more variegated ethnos. But why? My friend, who is writing a novel based on the life of Job, wants to know. And, because I cannot give him Rorty's answer, I give him my own: Because.

Because the sky is empty and heat lightning strokes the parched hillsides.

Because fires sweep into the valleys, charring the houses of poor and wealthy alike.

Because philosophy is not a science and science is a story for the mad.

Because, when Jean-Paul Sartre looked at the world in 1935, he saw that people, in order to survive, would have to become responsible in the absence of God and so he dispensed with the self and its past which was full of excuses.

49

And Emerson, strolling the clapboard streets of Boston, wanting to declare America free, once and for all, of Europe's tedious argument, inadvertently liberated us for cable TV, *The National Enquirer,* amusement parks, lottery tickets, and Madonna.

Because Socrates, who kept insisting he was ignorant, nonetheless spent his life teaching and seducing his students.

Because knowledge is power and wisdom unapproachable.

And Rorty, standing at the end of 10,000 years of the pursuit of Truth, deciding that sentences are perhaps acts of the mind with no correspondence to what is "real," rises from the table where that game is being played and goes to work.

The Wheel of Appetite

What should the birds mean, huddled in the eaves as the wind stretches its story over the yard? As the dust hums of barrenness to the grass? As darkness sets up its filigreed tent? Why does the raven peer into our rooms and shrug? Or tumble from flight as if shot? An omen or the predictable loopings of chaos? The patternlessness that achieves elegance only in distance or memory. Like our lives.

When my friend left her husband the night seemed full of a purple sheen that kept drawing itself out of the darkest corners. The future kept snapping at her, snarling and hissing and backing into its hole. All the lies she'd carefully assembled shifted beneath her. Trust was a paper boat she'd floated on an ocean. No sentence could accommodate her despair. *I am no one, I am no one,* she sang. She was eighteen she was forty. The years were an ellipsis she could not complete.

What was missing? Two cars, a house, enough furniture to seat their several friends. Shades to thwart the curious. Food and a dish to slide under it. Figurines and paintings they'd shopped their weekends for. Emblems of togetherness, their compromises, extremes. Already emptied of their histories, assertions and passions, their tenderness. His records, her books. The unstrung guitar, the unpainted canvas. The yearly hobbies abandoned in the attic. The self-help books glowering and cajoling from the nightstand. The television bristling and crackling in the darkened room, speaking of failure to the unconverted.

The bitten nails, the lost argument of the flesh. A device to strap across the stomach's drowse, a system of filters and conduits to divert the elegant, poisonous smoke from the lungs.

The trained kindnesses and seductive hands. The latest disease and its expensive cure. The groomed finger of light pointing out her failure to achieve happiness. She could snap it off from any point in her den. She could watch the shadow slide across the adobe wall. Or was the light failing?

And what of the finches? They hopped oblivious along the wall, chattering of nothing to the air. The bright reddishness at their throats gave a momentary pleasure each time she drank it, but the meaninglessness terrified her. In each mouth, a bit of straw for the nest. Each bird, an appetite with wings. They mated indiscriminately, closeting their young in the junipers. None feared routine or flew resolutely into the bumpers of cars. None dropped the straw to elope with the promise of continual ease and delight.

Ease and continual delight. Here were the recipes, the spring fashions, the CD with its strummed guitars and its new song about loneliness and the failures of language. Here was the new movie about dying. A dance to make us look like machines; a machine to make us look like dancers. A device to obliterate the meadowlark's song, the wind's idiotic duet with the cottonwoods.

The wheel of appetite spins like a gyroscope in our groins. In our stomachs and eyes. From the first apple to the glittering Porsche. But to sit among the piñon and sage. To let the wind blow and dust settle on the skin and not think of erosion and death, of loss and stillness and the closets of our unhappiness. To watch the scrub jays hurtle across the open spaces and lodge in the thick fur of the piñons and not see them as evil but as embodiments of a singular, fierce, and manageable appetite.

The Hawk. The Road. The Sunlight After Clouds.

Say you are driving in Vermont, spring, the sun emerging from clouds, the road twisting among farmhouses and farmhouses converted into country homes for the wealthy, and a bird breaks out of the woods into the air above and just in front of your car, startles, catches himself, spreads his rufous wings and his broadly striped tail and becomes a hawk, a broad-winged hawk.

You have been driving five hours and, until this moment, have deadened yourself with the radio's ragged rock—a half-dozen chords and the lyrics: "I love her but now she's shopping with him," "The refrigerator's open and the beer is gone." Some cross between pleasure and pain where noise meets noise: the guitar's doodle and thwack, the tires' rabble, the whistle from the window that won't quite shut.

You are leaving a place where you could not quite make a living, heading to a place where you will not quite make a living. You are, of course, me. You (here I mean you) are probably relieved to be out of that car, although you can, if you were born in America at midcentury, no doubt recall being in similar circumstances.

I am writing this for you, though I hope others—Mexicans, Swedes, Egyptians, Americans of future and past generations—can also imagine driving a car, seeing a bird, a hawk, a small hawk not ten feet away through the windshield, beautiful the way it catches itself, acknowledging your presence by veering slightly.

I want you to see this because seeing it myself is meaningless, lonely. I don't want to be alone in my seeing. Though the sight lightened me, somehow, made me forget the pains in my back, the dull throbbing in my temples. And it was a way of keeping time, of remembering: The Trip Before the Hawk / The Trip After the Hawk.

Still, it must seem a trivial thing to those struggling with arid land, government oppression. But I can imagine the sight of a bird lightening even those burdens. The right bird in the right place—aloft and weightless or nearby, perched. The different meanings there. Robins roosting or gulls drifting. My year-old daughter watches the crows and gulls returning to roost at dusk. "Bird," she says, tapping the glass. "Bird."

And I suspect that Noah's dove was notable not because it carried an olive branch, but simply because it was a bird, aloft, the freedom it promised the captives of the crowded, rocking ark, the hope embodied there, the feeling of hope, how we are lightened by hope, how even the soul seems to be birdlike— winged and able to sing.

Can you understand this, withering mothers and children, South Africans, Salvadorans, you there starving, you sealed in the box in darkness, you with your genitals wired to the generator? I saw this bird and it made me feel better. I just wanted to tell you about it. Can you imagine my freedom?

I was driving, yes *driving* from one state to another. My wife was in another car. Yes, we had two cars. We stopped to eat twice. My daughter was smiling at strangers. Can you imagine that? Now I am sitting on the porch of a lakeside cottage. I can see everyone, and everyone can see me and I am utterly safe. I am making a list of the birds I see:

<pre>
      black-throated blue warbler
             phoebe
           barn swallow
          northern oriole
              crow
</pre>

I have a little money, some food, and this house I'm renting. I have read some history. There are always wars. There are always two literatures—the literature of the oppressor, the literature of the oppressed. The literature of the oppressor is always stylistically superior (he has more time); the literature of the oppressed is always more urgent (he has less time).

Rain falls gently on the lake; the coffee cools at my elbow. Across the water, a man cuts logs with a chainsaw. Above my head, nestling phoebes faintly chirp their hunger songs. Once, I was driving in Vermont and a hawk hung briefly over the hood of my car. It was beautiful—the hawk, the road, the sunlight after clouds.

I have written about that hawk, about seeing that hawk. In the days to come I will write about similar incidents: the small joys and miseries, the tribulations of love in a privileged society, the speckled flanks of a brook trout, the things my daughter says. Wouldn't you? Given the time and freedom. Wouldn't you?

III. The Ochre World: A Sequence

poplars are on fire after Van Gogh
—George Steiner

The Levelled Site of the Page

In the broom closet, in the writer's nook, in the wires
    inhabiting the night.
Not the solvents and brews; the levelled site of the page.
Some staring at the sun, where the sun had been.
If you must, then. If you cannot help yourself.
The colonel, walking with a limp, sounded like a woman in a
    jingle dress.
The golden eagle brushing its wingtips against the cliff.
The moon. The full moon. The moon at perigee drawing
    potatoes out of the rich humus. Potatoes emerging like
    turtles out of a long hibernation.
In some Scandinavian countries, ideas wear woolen skirts in
    winter.
In summer, stars fall over the countryside like salt.
Not even the president, began one of my grandmother's
    favorite sayings.
The truck veered like a swooning boxer.
The moon swayed. The. Moon. Swayed.
Dogs rooted in the garbage. Dogs howled.
Not a single one. Over. Over my. Over my dead.
Over my dead body, under the sounds inhabiting the wire,
    under the wires inhabiting the night.
Not the solvents and brews.
Sniffing the air. The air full of howls and night sounds.
In Moenkopi, with my friend Cedric, among the stone walls,
    near the spring, beside the fields, under the July sun.
In with among near beside under.
If you must. If you cannot help yourself.
An ant suspended in amber. A coat of arms.
A waltz.
A held note.

The Held Note of the Past

Our voices go into the night, but the night happens outside the voices, outside the languages we have for the night. Not magic, not the solvents and brews, but the mystery of the dogs, the mystery of the night air that is full of the unsayable—the language, untranslatable, of howls and night sounds. And place is no tether. Location no security. When I was in Moenkopi, I felt a quickening loneliness, an openness. Felt more acutely on the drive over the mesas. The presence of the unnameable. The desire, then, to be located. The prepositions by which we locate ourselves in time and place. The failure of those words. Therefore, writing as an attempt to establish ourselves some where, some time. And the past, the invented past—ant in amber, coat of arms, waltz. The forms by which we try to plant ourselves in history, in story. The held note of the past in whose duration we try to live.

The Eye of Delight

In some segments, where there is an eye.

Not delight. Not stormclouds accreting. Not the darkened
    valley.

Freud. Jung.

Here is the story which means a) life is terrible b) life is
    terrible but.

A hummingbird gluing lichens to its nest: red, yellow, green,
    etc.

A tire with another four thousand miles on it.

Jung, then. Not Freud.

The carolers held their books, but the snow was too thick.

The wind too strong.

Frightening, the toads, in their relentless lapping of
    mealworms.

Across the canyon, one could see the adobe house O'Keeffe
    painted in, "lived" in.

But not that mountain. Not that cloud.

The eye of delight, the very eye.

Stormclouds and rain—god's hair sweeping over the mesas.

Not the horned toad. Not car-in-flames.

The children.

The mountain on which.

Quickly now, go, and do not return without the head of X,
    the eyes of Y.

Or do not go.

Wind. Wind. Wind.

Blue wind. Yellow wind. Red wind with its messages.

Seeds. Eagles. Small finches with their parcels, with their feet
    curled up, tucked up. With their feet. And their downy
    breasts.

Cold, the wind, and the branches thick with snow.

A Dazzling Incomprehensibility

And beauty attends the story at every moment. Look away from the destroyed motorcycle, the dying boy, and the birds are singing, the hummingbird is "decorating" its nest. The world, then, is not a site upon which to build, but a made place. Jung, not Freud. For now. For now, the carolers cannot sing, cannot see the words, the words which want to be uprooted from the page, which want to be sent into the world. Which want to be sent into the wind, which will tear the syllables out of the carolers' mouths. *O'Keeffe*, a friend told me as we stared across the valley at the adobe house tucked into the redrock canyon, *painted the sacred Apache mountain over and over*. She must have known of her transgression. That the sacred must not be fixed. That the image can drain power. Where, then, is the eye of delight? Once, in O'Keeffe country, we watched a storm sweep across the peaks. "God's hair," my four-year-old daughter called the rain falling from such height onto such heights. The story, untold, behind the image, involves the gods and their relationship to humans. The story, untold, is about the dazzling incomprehensibility of nature. About the fantastical—horned toad, car-in-flames. The children. The violated mountain. The story, untold, is about power and fear. About the orders to kill and blind. About the refusal of those orders.

A Sheen, A Radiance

Augury and the big beat.

Because. Because. Because.

The sun's penis swinging in the solar wind.

Two men in an ochre world, in a world lit by sunlight
through a screen of bamboo branches.

The truth as we know it: Crows huddled in the cottonwoods.

The back arched. The woman's back arched.

Not sex, but a dive into.

Into memory, the dependent clause.

And outside the sentence: The balloon drifts. Drifts and
shudders. Red over green hemlocks.

Red over green, and the sun pressing its face into the plowed
field.

The guitarist setting off harmonics like bombs with his thin
fingers.

Lost in the night concert air.

Lost in the stream, the brook, the freshet, the rivulet.

Lost.

In an ochre world, in the dust swirled by a circular wind—
two men.

Not brothers, though linked by disaster.

In memory, in the dependent clause.

In the rich bottomlands, in the mist-webbed bogs.

Where corn and squash grow bountiful.

Where yellow and green.

Where the woman arched her back, in memory.

In memory, and the red balloon.

The ochre world.

Brutal Squares

The poem arrives emblazoned in language. The poem arrives festooned with rhythm and a sense of completion. It is half of the rainbow. The rainbow slowly materializing. The rainbow that grew until it touched the meadows beside the river. The rainbow that my daughter and I followed until it fell, barely visible—a sheen, a radiance—around the black and white cows grazing disconsolately beside the mud-engorged Pecos River. Augury, therefore. The poem a dry lake. Words like water. And the big beat—rock 'n' roll, the metronomic swings of the moon, tidal pulse. And the child's epistemology: *Because*. The navigable, the *companionable*, world. Father sun, mother earth, and the story told in many cultures of the sun's penis. The Ojibwa story of the woman impregnated by the sun. In the fields, among the unfurling leaves.

But this dream takes place in the brutal squares, in the hard pan, in the terror-inflected markets. Southeast Asia and the pages of history flutter in a dry wind. In a dream, and two men emerge like lungfish from drought. Memory cracks the mud-crust of daily life. Inside, the war-scarred child. Inside, in the moment preserved like a diamond of pain. Inside, the ochre world. Inside, sunlight and shadow. But the men want clarity. The men want certainty. The men want, therefore, death. Which is the usual, the order of the day. A clear winner. They torment each other with their own disappointments. *You,* they are saying. *You live in a golden light and are untouched by beauty.*

Meanwhile, the crows. Meanwhile, the world's desolate clarity. Meanwhile, the woman. Her back arched as if. In memory, *into* memory, into *language. In language—where desire swims with just its eyes showing.* Meanwhile, outside the sentence.

Meanwhile, color and festival. Meanwhile, the sun, the big beat. Woodstock, and Hendrix returning the anthem into the poisonous air of its birth. Notes swirl in the rich farmland. *In an ochre world*—two men, veterans, veterans of violence and anger, veterans of what the Romanian poet, in a seminar, called "the occult workings of governments." If they cannot have the world they want, they want no world. *Because.* And the corn and squash. And the world saying, *live.* And the world saying, *in memory, the red balloon, the woman.* Listen: *This anger is deep and so is joy.*

Tokens from a Lost World

In the curl, crash, and wash over sand.

In the foam of never-was.

From the top of the ponderosa: the mesa, black clouds
 pulsing with static.

In Brazil, in the Amazon, anthropologists have learned such
 and such.

Tokens from a lost world. From nothing-is-lost.

At this time. At this place. At this juncture of nine A.M. and a
 kitchen. At this coffee cup, this sunlight.

"But who will come? And from where?"

In the gypsy camp, a man raps and batters a blonde guitar. A
 woman draws a scarf across her shoulders, turns her face
 from her imagined lover.

The red-tailed hawk, whose cry is often mistaken for, is often
 used to simulate, in, for example, Hollywood westerns,
 the cry of the eagle.

The clamor of an engine breaks the stillness of sunrise.

What use has the sun for imagination?

The horses shudder their fur, snort, and thump their feed
 barrels.

Why should these prepositions keep us from the truth? The
 president held his coffee like a beggar's tin cup and spoke
 frankly.

Geese across the blind face of the moon. Blind as a metaphor
 for unseeing. Face as a metaphor for loneliness.

Not the gulf between fact and its allies.

Not the thick quilt of language.

The child at play in the aspen grove.

The animals talking to each other with human voices.

A Wave

A wave, then. In Rilke, the "new warm receding wave on the sea of the heart" is an emblem for absence, the going-away at the center of presence. The never-was arriving with the now. So we climb higher. We see farther. Further darknesses. In that dark cloud, the flashes of static are an emblem for memory. Perhaps. This is a reading. Each segment is a reading. Writing is the word's way of assuring its own survival. We keep thinking the answer lies in the past. We keep thinking, *If we only dig deeper.* We keep thinking, *To establish our being. Go back, go back, our true selves lie on the raft made of reeds, in the bower formed by an arch of bone.*

> Twentieth-century Americans kept searching for human nature's roots in the deep past while, ironically, building a future on the promise of an "unfixed" human nature. The theory of a fixed human nature dominated the sociopolitical spheres while artists and social scientists were uncomfortable allies in the struggle to hold open the possibilities for change.

"But change"—my friend says it in a poem—"is the cruellest savior." And that is where we are, that is the light we see by. It is a dim light, from a nearly full moon that casts faint shadows as we move from the *portal* to the garden, as we stand under the mimosa-like tree among the buzzing yucca moths. But that is poetry, a child's game. That is desire and artifice.

The Valley

The people moved to the valley because they wanted to keep being surprised by weather. The children were told stories about the wonders beyond the hills. Later, the young men ventured beyond the hills and saw the endless, empty plains. Bitterly disappointed, they camped above the village and sat until the fire died and then sat some more, silent, under the cup-shaped moon. In the morning, they hiked into the village and told stories of great herds of white horses; bountiful crops of corn, squash, grapes; snakes that foretold the future; molten rock that sent great spires of steam hissing into the sky; the seven moons that circled the earth—a belt of angels holding hands—and the promise they heard sung down from the heavens: That they were the chosen ones and would outlive all their enemies. That they would live forever in that bountiful land. The people of the village cheered and wept. Some spoke of leaving the village, of moving onto the plains. The young men became alarmed. Then the wisest one spoke: "All of these wonders will be ours, provided we are virtuous. Provided we are patient. These are the words of the angels. We have brought them to you and you must have faith. Those without faith, those who attempt to look upon the angels and their paradise, will be denied eternal life." With that, life returned to normal in the village. The clouds continued to pour suddenly over the west rim, the seasons were mild or harsh, but the stories in the village changed, and the elders' faces were radiant with wisdom and promise.

"The Woman"

The woman in the García Lorca poem dies of desire, dies luminously, and we are not allowed to feel pity. The poem is a kind of dance meant to attract and repel. A dance composed of seductiveness and stomping. What we want is not the eagle's cry, but the illusion of the eagle crying. The callers were "outraged" when "it was revealed" that their favorite "woman," the one who knew exactly what they needed to hear on the 900 line, was not a woman at all. One man, who wanted to marry his need to "her" voice, threatened to sue. In the "studio audience"—distinguished from the television audience by its apparent presence—the women laughed bitterly, without pity. Realism is based on conventions and conventions are based on desire. The desire for calm, for example, broken by the clamor of an engine, which is a desire for movement. But the imagination can obliterate almost any paradise. And still the world, the solid world, drifts, unmoved, beyond us. Beyond us, the horses in their absolute forms. Beyond us, the gasses burning and bursting, sending unimaginably hot flames into the unimaginable emptiness. So we return to the comforts of language, to the pleasantly manipulative language of power and exerted force. And, sometimes, the beauty, the indeterminate layerings of image. Geese. Moon. Loneliness. Not the gulf. Not the gaps and certainties, the word hanging around the neck of the actual, but this innocence, this childish play, these voices given, given up, or listened to and granted form, this tenderness portioned equally among the gathered creatures.

Interiors

The unstated theme is distance. The unstated theme is the distances that live inside language like termites deep in the beams of a house. When the inspector finally arrived, he tapped at the surface and the beams crumbled. The treatment was costly but necessary. The men wore parts of their uniforms, remnants of a former discipline—this man wore a crumpled hat, this the green pants, this one the tattered shirt with the emblem announcing his allegiance. They knocked and drilled. They dug. They injected poisons. Carpenters jacked up the roof, slid new beams into place. When the homeowner signed the contract, the man in the tweed jacket and tie assured him and reassured him. But the man couldn't help hearing the motions, the infinitesimal creepings inside the beams. At night, while he slept, he knew the dark interiors were filling with light.

God's "Malevolent Eye"

A way to explain. Not history.
Not names and dates.
Not a famished thrusting after facts.
Not the bushwacked, the poorly formed.
An orgy of labybugs, a rotten log.
In the sump of flax.
In the tall orders, the lackey's smile.
A single goshawk in a thousand square miles of timber.
No, *lumber.*
The ozone hole like God's eye.
Like God's "malevolent eye."
When the famous professor paused between a statement of
    fact and the ensuing theory, a hundred watches beeped
    the new hour.
On the freeways, cars pushed their small envelopes of sound
    or tormented the night with their huffing rap.
Eagle sparrow robin starling ovenbird.
In the long recession, in the stupefied night.
Thermometer in the mouth of the dying day.
Everyone crowded around the counter, unable to locate the
    bar code.
The astronauts, lacking prepositions, tumbled uncontrollably.
Then there was a party—brief, impassioned moments, a
    smattering of handsome clothing, expressions of genuine
    surprise and mock delight.
The miserable, we soon discovered, are much like the
    delighted, only more miserable.
Later, we stumbled out in search of new blurred genres to
    conquer.

A Party of Sorts

Like sound, history moves among us. Like the tide filling the salt marsh. Tongues of water and, above the water, the rushes and grasses, the redwing calling out of memory, chanting its unchanged . . . . Not history, but the story the mountain tells. Once, while hiking in Montana, I came upon the swarmed ladybugs. Once, in the sexual slough of Anglo-Saxon, in the rich tapestry of vowels. Not history with its privileged observers. Not history with its elaborate plot. Not history with its one swollen ankle, its shining cities in the storm-enthralled night. When the goshawk announced itself, when it perched among the stultifying prepositions, the environmentalists called it toward presence, called it out of the past—Old English *gos-hafoc*, "goose-hawk"—into a dangerous present. Goose hawk, goshawk, perched in the sentence. Perched among resources. And, above us, the new God of Accommodations, twitching and barking, drifting in a Nembutal haze. Sound moving among us like the ocean rising into the salt marshes, like history pouring into the cities, like a mist, a webbed mist spreading over the gullies and ravines in the hills above the Mississippi's headwaters, Winona, Minnesota, 1980. My wife and I were driving to Montana, were entering the West. Before ozone, before the goshawk, before words became letters became snakes slipping onto the ledges to warm themselves in late spring. The sudden tautology surprised everyone. The professor placed his wine glass on the silver tray, coughed softly into his handkerchief. *Ad hoc*, he thought, and that triggered other fallacies. *Sui generis, fin de siècle, bon appétit, apéritif.* This was a party of sorts, and above them, the astronauts. Try as he might, no one could feel his way onto the illuminated streets—Manhattan, and the woman, placing her doctoral dissertation in the shopping cart, watched her hand break into a dozen hands on the concrete sidewalk.

Ravel

In that piece by Ravel, where nothing keeps happening.
Where subtlety achieves the grandeur of a semicolon.
And now these crows stalking the courtyard—hard, swift pop
    stars of the ponderosa.
All image and quickness. A dazzle of surfaces.
A jet glinting westward; a basketball spinning through the
    hoop.
"Pray," he said, watching the cliffs above Jemez Pueblo, "for
    everything that moves."
Pray that what is *is* what is.
Pray that and to whom. Or what.
Side to side is the skunk's way of walking.
It appears as a sheen on the darkness, a bristling sheen and a
    line that is not exactly a line, but more like a sine wave.
More like smoke, windblown from a chimney.
When my brother rode out, across the lawn, his motorcycle
    was like the purring, amplified, of a cat.
Minutes later, the unimaginable kept circling around the
    words the voice spoke into the phone.
Minutes later, in the afternoon sunlight, among the chrome
    and apple red.
Minutes later, after the swerve and crash.
If only occurred. What if. Then the silence after.
Silence of tires rolling, of afternoon sunlight and the mute
    silences it illuminated.
Silence of bumper-glint and polished fender. Silence of knots
    adjusted.
Silence of all the moments before and the moment after.
Like that piece by Ravel, where nothing keeps happening.

Sunlight on Stucco

Sunlight on stucco,
white lilies.
Clustered speakers
above the empty fairgrounds.

Before the Rains

Before the rains: The earth cracked like a hand.
Fear, racism, and the fiddle's lovely screech and squawk.
The earth turned its pockets inside-out and shrugged.
A handful of notes shaken in a cup and rattled onto the
    mahogany bar.
The arc of a missile, the arc of a missile.
Because they felt it they put it in their song.
Herons stalked the rice paddies.
One foot lifted like a lily. A lily hanging from a broken stalk.
The moon set loose above the mountains.
The film was beautiful but racist.
If I told you to slaughter the villagers would you slaughter the
    villagers?
The child clutching the woman is no longer a child. Nor is
    the woman a woman.
How lovely the dance and colorful. How carefully, how
    meticulously wrought, the image.
They could learn, the expert was saying, how to respect
    difference, but they would remain—at some deep level—
    unmoved.
When the monsoons flooded the land, the snakes found dry
    ground in the abandoned village.

Damage

And weren't you always moved by the poignant damage? The child clutching at the woman's dress while the soldiers march through the bomb-torn village. The mother watching the limp body of her drowned son loaded onto a sling. She touches the cold hand that flops from the sling, swinging joylessly in the cold drizzle. And maybe you step into the gray dawn, and the moon, floating over the mesa, fills you with a lovely anguish. Or you lie down with your husband and enter the walled kingdom of touching. Or you find your way into language, this fragmentation that, we have discovered, can approximate wholeness. This style that has the aspect of, the *heft* of, substance. A density difficult to breathe in. A smoke-filled room. The old man curled pitifully in the corner. Dead—a picture to take. There, but for the grace of accident. There, but for the safety precautions we've taken. There, and the smoke drifts and the aperture. The smoke. The sunlight pushing through the shattered glass, pushing a column into the smoke, igniting the particulates. The man labelled *dead*. Terror giving way to resignation giving way to peace—landscape with poplars; fruit on a table; man, dead, in a smoke-filled room. The musicians kept playing the same three chords and the people kept applauding. The singer kept entering the same story filled with the same vowels and the people kept applauding. They were delighted by the shapes misery achieved. The sparks of woe leaping from the guitarist's fingers.

A Closet Full of Excruciations

That afternoon in America when you were assuming what I
    was assuming.
The waves struck at an odd angle and rolled like a blind with
    a hitch in it.
O my little ones, my oysters, my clams.
O my winsome adjectives.
Lightning then thunder then tea and scones.
The coal fire in the stove, the fig in the greenhouse.
The abandoned motel demanding interpretation.
New shoes and a big dog. An engine wanting adjustment.
Let it go. In memory, the gulls are rapid over the scrub oaks.
In memory, like something thrown from a fire.
In the "technopop" song, a man keeps returning to a
    restaurant, a man keeps ascending the subway stairs into
    the light of into the glare of.
Then the notes fall off the guitar like drops of flame.
A closet full of excruciations. A bank of candles and a breeze.
Then the future in its subcompact. The future downshifting
    to make the meager hills.
The sand kept trying to bury the grass which kept etching its
    name on the sand.
Near Deal Island, caught on a bridge while the tide lowered,
    "the speaker" watched a harrier "mapping the wind with
    its wings."
There was a way to continue, but first we had to watch the
    local cut a plug of blubber out of a beached pilot whale's
    neck.
There were other costs, too, but they kept turning into poetry.

A Desperate Longing for Presence

The unstated theme is absence. Heidegger spoke of a feeling of "thrown-ness," a feeling of "already-being-in-the-world," of context. A feeling, Rilke reminds us, of already-passing-away. The unstated theme of absence. The waves rolling, but the hitch become emblem, become "moments out of time," moments slowed or stopped by the mind, by memory. The outlines of trees were softened, as if they'd been soaking a long time. The birds "sang," though the word keeps promising a human joy. The swallows "twittered" as they looped over the greening grasses. I could say whales rolled and spumed in the harbor, but there were hours when nothing happened, when the merest wheeze of a warbler, when the wind just fluttering the scrub oaks, when the quotidian earth rolled *like a sleepy whale,* when the imagination embellished a desperate longing for presence, for the thicket of memory and event that creates the illusion of, the feel of, being-in-the-world. Mostly, though, emptiness wanted its story told. Mostly, emptiness wandered the dunes like a lost dog. In one valley between dunes, the wind kept sorting the sand from the pebbles. Such beauty—a mound of mottled pebbles, sand, scrub oaks, stunted pines, more sand. When the hikers came upon the abandoned motel, they understood it as a metaphor for their inner lives—the shuffleboard courts, the snack bar, the empty pool. The carnival of absence and longing. The narrative of love which is the most powerful story in a culture without local wars, without the spirit-walk.

> The poet went into the woods and returned with the words to his song. He carved them into a wooden shield and went off to battle. Good fortune followed him like a faithful dog. Arrows bounced off the shield. When he threw his spear, it struck the enemy in the breast and was returned to him. As he approached the enemy camp, he noticed a beautiful

woman lounging, head down, beside a stream. He began to sing his song. She lifted her head and turned to face him. She looked at him, and he forgot the words. Without thinking, he turned his shield to read the words carved there. The woman leaped to her feet, swinging a sword. As she approached, the poet could see the words carved into her sword. They were written in a language foreign to him, but in the instant before she struck him, he understood what they meant.

There should be a long solo here, the glissando's elision of experience, the details bypassed in favor of a shimmering vibrato, a moan, a cry contagious as a yawn. There should be humor and cruelty. Change. The panther of memory stalking its cage. When zoologists first attempted to release the rehabilitated mountain lion in the Gila Wilderness, it sniffed the air once and hurried back into its cage. In the 50s, when the American comedians arrived in the aboriginal village, the elders mistook them for holy men.

A Letter to the Future

A letter to the future: In this period you have named _____.
In these times of voluptuousness and pain.
In the waning days of the twentieth century.
The men, failing to express their tenderness and grief, went
    into the woods to bang on drums and assemble their
    "medicine bundles."
Sun moon dismemberment death. Robins singing themselves
    to sleep.
What were we missing? In Heather's video, a black-gloved
    hand.
In Heather's video a tiny model of the earth is rolled
    randomly in a black-gloved hand.
It could have been my hand. It could have been yours.
We keep failing to make a religion of absence.
We keep "meaning well."
How can a hummingbird? How can these eggs the size of, in
    the literature, lima beans?
Or the night filled with yucca moths.
When my friend asked why a man couldn't simply hold up a
    chart assembled from the miserable facts and be elected,
    the answer was inevitable and ominous.
Who would pay for the chart? Where would he hold it?
The nest itself was formed of a foamy orange substance the
    books called "plant down."
Then the birds glued lichens with spider webs to the outside.
Intended to camouflage the nest, the red and green lichens
    achieved, instead, a kind of existential grandeur.
In crisp autumn air, in pale morning sunlight, in mist rising
    from the heating grates on the White House lawn, a
    nation of street people rose poetically to its feet.

The Signature

In Los Angeles, in 1992, the year the ghost of Columbus stalked the Pueblos, the year Americans chose sides, four policemen were acquitted of pummelling a black man. The video showed it clearly, but the video was a video. You could rent them for 49 cents. You could sit back and watch the brutal, simplified world. The evil. The good. This was a service we were provided. Occasionally, a man or woman would stand up from the pages of a novel so mixed, so torn by events, so noble and so battered by conscience that we couldn't recognize him as human except in small groups of the studious. Because a white man once called him a goddamn injun, the young poet denied himself all hope. Because the grocer was Asian, because he was inclined to capitalism and hard work, the neighbors tormented him. The black man who, even at forty-five years old, was beautiful when he drove the baseline, spinning—*his shoes squeaking, the basketball thumping hard into the waxed hardwood floor*—and stuffing the ball behind his head, had no sense of his beauty off the court. Failure soaked into his body as he sat on the locker room bench. The gray walls of failure, the rusted and battered lockers of failure, the waters of failure, hot then cold. In the streets of failure, he walked in his failed clothing. *Spinning, then, his shoes squeaking the basketball thumping. Spinning, and the signature his body left on the air.*

The Ritualized Forms

Anything is possible, but not everything can be spoken of.
If we want to get from A to B.
If we want to wear party hats and make noises by placing one
    hand under the opposite arm and squeezing.
Anything is possible, but the swallow flits over the cornfield.
Anything is possible as the woman rises before the man,
    pushes the curtains aside and lets the sunrise fill her.
Anything and the suddenness of two herons low over the
    cornfields.
Two herons emerging from or merging into.
Two herons sculling through a sky of language. Sky full of
    5:50 A.M., kids asleep, mother ill, and a handful of bills.
Not tragedy, but an American dailiness.
Here in the Age of (choose one).
Here in the flux of memory.
Dear Future Reader: What has become of coherence? What
    new names have you found for events?
How do you explain A then B then C?
My personal life is of no interest. Still, there are these losses,
    these joys.
My daughter inventing voices for her plastic horses; poetry;
    the swished basketball; the consideration of ideas; a
    flicker's cry in the dawn.
My wife dressing in muted light.
The pleasures of culture, the ritualized forms.
This is how life was—for some, sometimes, in America, in the
    final moments of the twentieth century.

Meanwhile

Meanwhile, in Juarez. In South L.A. Harlem. The Bronx. Meanwhile, in the alleys of D.C. Beirut. Nepal. *Meanwhile: The terror of that word.* When the soldier sodomized the twelve-year-old girl, she thought he'd shoved a bayonet up inside her and that she was dying. *It's spring, and the girls are decorating the neighbor's dog with ribbons.* On the streets of L.A., two black men dragged a white truck driver onto the pavement and kicked and beat him, cracking his skull. *The irises in bloom—so delicate, almost erotic.* Because he was albino and because the legends held he was bewitched, the young warriors took him into the mountains, beheaded him and cut off his fingertips. *When the beginning poet wrote "blue sky caresses the mesa," the professor "bristled."* The tattooed dwarf, wearing a cutoff denim jacket, wandered among the five-year-old girls at the mall. *In the morning, my daughter, waking from the land of dreams where everything is in question, insists that we call her "Grayce." No pet names, no endearments—just Grayce.* In Monet's version of La Grenouillère, suffering is off the canvas, not to be found among the bathers, the islanded forms. Even the man walking the narrow plank is poised, steady; he has *all the time in the world.* Even the dark boats that deliver our gaze to the man on the plank do not contain the blindfolded, mutilated bodies. Do not contain Picasso's *Vollard,* a man so invaded by geometry, so riddled by the angular vicissitudes of 1910, that his contemplative pose has become demonic. He no longer thinks Great and Noble Thoughts; he presides dispassionately over the fire in his lap.

> In one theory of dreaming, the brain generates images randomly and a "story-making" region tries to "make sense" of them, "using" its innate or culturally developed sense of causality and story to protect "us" from meaninglessness. In

this theory two men arrive in an ochre world, two anony-
mous men arrive unbidden, and the dreamer, a kind of
author, invents their lives, animates them, "informs" them.
What this means—*clubs raised, in black and white, the time
blinking in the corner*—what this means, then, and this is
the source of our error, is that there are countless stories
being generated, countless versions. Such terror and beau-
ty, such a struggle for language and power.

*The lilies shimmer in a slight breeze; their silvery leaves form a
visual glissando.* And Rodney King, a "black man," an "Afro-
American," a "Gorilla in the Mist," who was struck 56 times
by police billy clubs in Los Angeles, stands before the cameras,
nearly sobbing, and asks for an end to the violence. *The girls,
only five years old, thought the dwarfed man was cute; therein lay
the source of the fear, therein lay the fathers' terror.* "Blue sky. The
mesa." *Caress, the professor insisted, when deployed in this sen-
tence, creates a hackneyed, sentimental image. The sky cares noth-
ing for the mesa. The sky and the mesa care nothing for you.*
Okay, then, said the student: "The blue sky tore at the mesa's
throat." *Much better, said the professor. Much, much better.*

The Common Man

(In petto)

He was writing for the common man, but the common man was sleeping in his favorite chair, was dragging his bread through the yolk. He was writing for the common man, but Michael Jordan was peripateticating spectacularly through the crepuscular den. He was writing for the common man, but the six-pack, the film starring the former bodybuilder, the *ha ha* of pure evil having its face thrust into the gaping machinery, the unalloyed pleasure of the home team (good) versus the visitors (evil). He was writing for the common man, secretly nursing his contempt for the common man. Wanting to *improve* him. Wanting to make him see, to acknowledge, to embrace the murkiness of human motives. To make him squirm in his favorite chair. To make him awaken in the claws of a dream. To make him walk out into the morning of fog-webbed pastures, creaking milk trucks, children called into the open with their readers and lunch boxes, the horses whickering in their undersized corrals. He was writing for the common man, but the common man was balancing his coffee between his legs, was sitting between two masons in a red dump truck. Had his feet up on the tool bag, his knees leaned far right, anticipating the long throw into third.

He was writing for the common man, secretly thinking *all is lost*. But the sun in the east, the moon still floating, the *larval* moon still floating in the western sky. The common man already out, walking his property line. Already out, waxing the Camaro with the common woman. Already out, stopping the BMW to pull prayer plumes from the road-killed bluebird— so delicate, wings half-extended, toes locked on (perched on) nothingness, the eyes shut tight against the promise of light and time. Already out, leaping from the scaffold—like a spider rappelling from ceiling to floor—vines wrapped tight around his ankles, then the sudden jolt, cloud of dust, the upside-down writhing, the whoops and shouts, the welcome into manhood. Already out, being struck by the poetries of trans-formation—sunlight fluttering on the truck hood, shadows puddled under junipers and piñons, crows arcing in the cymo-phanous dawn.

A Conspiracy of Lilacs

A conspiracy of lilacs at the window.
A clandestinary.
A racket of crows, luminous in dawn-light.
Finches concatenating above the cottonwoods.
A praxis of jackrabbits in the chamisa.
And, beside the snowmelt stream—the light-riven waters:
a clatter of squirrels.
A curmudgeon of picnickers lounging in graven sunlight.

A Broth

The star-nosed mole popped out of the earth like a log,
    flopped on its belly.
Its progress across the hardpan was like the progress of a canoe
    paddled by children.
In Vermont, in summer, my brothers and I commandeered
    our host's canoe and paddled into the starry night.
If meaning is a stew, these nouns, these verbs, this handful
    of adjectives must float in a broth before they can be
    digested.
Were we, that night, the lake's intelligence?
I could feel the cold broth, the turtles and fish, the *anacharis*
    and grasses swirling in the paddles' currents.
There was a night heron we never heard or saw. There was a
    loon, the promise of a loon.
There were books filled with color plates and maps.
Trouble was shouting and pointing in the inadequate
    spotlights.
We kept trying to be sufficient, kept projecting our
    competence into the room.
The chimney was somehow defective: Smoke poured through
    the electrical fixtures into the upstairs bedroom.
We were young and thought riding fast on the squalling
    motorbike would bring us closer to it.
The dog drank the gimlet and wobbled behind the couch. The
    raccoon licked our armpits, stuck its nose into our ears.
When psychologists decided that a happy childhood was
    possible and *necessary*, the whole nation became
    miserable.
Pleasure, we later learned, is sufficient, but must be alternated
    with long periods of hardship and denial.

Gold Card

Anger was best expressed by bellowing or a rapid double-
    picking on the bass strings.
The same phrases on the treble strings expressed
    mournfulness, grief, complaint.
In rapid succession: the stern professor, the jovial sportsman,
    the aggressive shopper.
Later, among a few sympathetic friends, he would project the
    bitterness of the wronged artist.
Some were lounging in the shade of their berets, "jotting" in
    their notebooks, drinking cappuccino, smoking French
    cigarettes, planning the revolution.
Others collected stamps, bred guppies, spray-painted graffiti
    on the concrete abutments.
All of this was encouraged.
The difficulty lay in somehow adapting the internal life
    (freedom) to social conditions (controls).
The camper under the carport; the lilacs blooming along the
    flagstone walk.
The looter, at first dismayed by his celebrity, soon adjusted
    and talked at length to the "foxy" reporter.
"These outsiders," he said. "They come into our
    neighborhood and take our money, our jobs."
"We're just doing a little shopping," another man shouted.
"Show her your Gold Card," a woman said, stepping through
    the shattered window.
The man, grinning, held up a brick.

Maxim

"From each according to his *vulner*ability;
to each according to his *greed*."

Heaven

Because heaven is a lake.
(A lake in the mountains.)
Because no paved roads should lead to the lake.
Because the trails should be, occasionally, treacherous.
Because worship requires a journey, "each step a word."
(The redbird in the tree, the horse in the valley.)
Because heaven is a lake with earthly trash down in it, with
    Budweiser and Burger King down in it.

Like Teeth

Singer's Gimpel, who seems perfectly reasonable (and wise) to
    me, was ridiculed by my students.

The meadowlark's song, while "beautiful," sounds like a
    malfunctioning gadget.

Changing subjects often and abruptly is one way to approach it.

The shudder of a jet on takeoff the mewing kitten the ninth
    born to the mother with eight teats circled and circled on
    the braided rug.

The chocolate milkshake the agonizing death.

Sunlight sunlight all day on the flower-shadowed stucco the
    boys placing the puppy into the box sitting on it the
    yelping.

Changing subjects often and abruptly may be one way of
    avoiding it.

"And we *are too* married," the woman managed through her
    wired-shut jaw, addressing the man with his leg in
    traction, addressing the bandage where his eyes would
    soon be. "And I *will* find the license."

They all wanted happiness, but could not agree on how best
    to achieve it.

When they discovered it, there were words all over it.

There were words down *in it, inside it. Like teeth.*

The Choir of the Actual

Because if you wanted the populace to behave, you had to negate the personal. If you wanted to impose a rigid—*military*—standard of behavior, you had to eliminate the self, which was full of impudence and vacillation, full, that is, of finches and lianas, wisteria bursting through wooden roofs. You must understand the dangers of the personal, the triumph of the shouted epitaph, the polarization, the rigidity—*the suddenness*—of opinion, the rejection of fact, the heart speaking on every corner, the heart speaking with its paper voice, the groin speaking with its paper voice, the stomach snarling its green snarl. We want this, we keep saying—*robinsong funnelling into the ear*—because we want it. We want this, we keep saying, because it is our right. We want this, we keep saying, and the fathers begin closing the galleries. We want this, we keep saying, and the fathers close the library doors. We want this, we keep saying—*as systems become more coherent and dominating, the arts become more hermetic and irrational*—and the fathers cough into their fists. We want this, we say—*finches, lianas, the crumbling infrastructure*—.

The people keep voting against intelligence, having seen—*but even the absence of ideas is an idea*—how ideas had enslaved them. The people keep voting with their hearts. "Trust your gut," they keep saying, as if inspiration is all one needs, as if the child could fashion the spear, track the jaguar, kill it, skin it, and carry it back to the village, as if the fire—*face pressed to the dirt, ear to the humming grasses*—were already burning there. "You know in your heart," they cry, but our hearts, too, are brimming with ideas, are bloated with wanting, with grief, with the need to speak and control.

We who cannot "leap the world's ties." We who long for the village of solitudes, the choir, not the "bare ruined choir"—*not the satisfactions of despair*—but the choir of the actual.

An American

"An American," Maximus wrote, "is a complex of occasions." And occasion—he would have known this—means to fall toward. To fall, as my wife and I fell, yesterday, toward coffee and a pleasant bookstore. As we fell, this morning, toward—in the local newspaper—a photograph of that bookstore. A photograph that must have been taken shortly before we arrived, that commemorates absence, that attends to everything not photographed—racks of magazines and books, crumbling adobe neighborhoods, telephone wires swaying with intense, casual conversations, memories swelling in the lilacs, flowing in the acequias, blood-spattered priests, jailed Pueblo leaders, cache of longing under the plaza grass, longing shaped into earrings and pottery, longing inscribed in racks of blankets, vested in theaters and galleries, scribbled in margins, entwined among arbors and portals. These Americans strolling the tax-sheltered streets of Santa Fe—*what is the real name of this place?*—are a complex of occasions. Are *falling*, and the photograph says, *Lovely.* And the photograph says, *Here is the generous life upwelling.* And the photograph says, *It is time to write the diary of your days. Among the gathered blossoms, in the morning courtyard, in the casual isolation you want to call privacy.*

Inside

—they kept capturing things in language and things kept
    escaping
they found words for what was happening they applied them
    to the video what was happening began to change
when they kept looking when the words held open the frames
    when the frames were seen through the words
when they sifted when the man when the time blinking when
    look into your hearts came up on the screen
he was far from his skin the horizon gone lights flooding over
    the arm coming down
all the pain inside where the light was too low where the blur
    might have been a scream
so far inside and everyone shaking hazards all around you
    could almost see the shadows
a vocabulary a lexicon of hazards smeared lights the indefinite
    approaching no words
circling on the freeways fear in a handful of dust the luxes so
    low now the traffic noises
and radio waves the static crackling how could we measure all
    this where would we take the readings
the light bouncing off the subject's face the bystanders waiting
    for a narrative waiting
you've got to understand what it's like out there the families
    waking up waiting up
nightgowns and slippers the coffee cup held in two hands the
    sound of slippers on linoleum
steam rising the scuffing sound of slippers long hair pushed
    back from the face
where it falls around the face the indefinite circling moving in
    shadows the money
the family values the man's drugs circulating in
    the neighborhood in the night air

the family values loaded into a van the family values kicking
    open the door
the ontological certainties kept shifting the relativity was not
    in the frame was in
each successive frame was in the story we were making up was
    the meaning in the image
in the closeup where the darkness was absolute and the light
    when they froze the image
when the close-up when the computer enhanced when you
    stood back you could see the beauty of it
the pattern the inevitability the softened edges of time of
    motion the nightstick
the hand must have been soaking a long time all the language
    gone the calligraphy stopped
the pulse the anger off the screen the word unfinished the
    agony passing into history
inside where the luxes are so low inside where the pain
    circles and circles on the dirt floor
shivering and twitching inside and the dust blowing inside
    where the words won't go
inside where the hazards where the nightsticks where the
    family values inside
but the light is so dim the torch the language the languages
    the window the lens scratched and scorched
inside where we keep the history the anger where we crush the
    berries where we keep drawing
the glyph the sign the hunters gathered around the bison
    the hunger the fear
circulating in the ochre pigments in the flame-opening down
    inside where we keep it
where we keep the pictures of it shivering and twitching and
    calling out in our sleep—

In the Sleep of Reason

In "The sleep of reason," the bats, whose true meaning might
    be delicacy, benign mystery—
a flight of hazards, their comic faces thrust into the night
      flowering cactus—
have become emblems of a dangerous chaos
because they fly in darkness,
because they should be birds and are not,
because they twitter like mice and have access to our secret
    skins,
because the *teeth*,
because they careen, dodging what we cannot see,
because their stories are told in the night, in caves,
because they are sudden, walk upside-down on wings,
because darkness is a kind of water,
because they can be upon us unexpectedly—like spiders and
    snakes, sickness and death,
because the unseen is a threat,
because hope and danger fly on the same wings,
because they stream out of the caves of our sleep and map us
    with inaudible languages,
because they listen to us without reproach,
because their voices return with news of the solid world,
because we are earthbound, light-locked, governed by
    appearance and theory,
while they navigate the solid, glistening darkness.

Oblivion's Mouth

To step. To step under. In the old stories. In the almost forgotten. In the stories effaced by language. Ravaged by history. Veiled by custom. In the old stories hiding inside the words.

> At the writer's conference they were talking about canons and someone said it was a legal term, but before that it was a religious term (and a legal term) from the Latin and before that the Greek which may be part of the problem. The word may not be related to the Spanish *cañon*, which began as *tube* and became *canyon* and *cannon* and entered the history of conquest, assisting thereby in ravaging the old stories.

But in those old stories, to step under the mistletoe—because the plant is epiphytic and is, therefore, of neither heaven nor earth—is to leave civilization behind and enter chaos, is, therefore, to enter the rotting, moss-delighted forest which surrounds the cave, a secret place, endless, cool and damp, an interior, inhabited by darkness and bats, oblivion's mouth, a lawless place where the branch is being dipped then lifted—*in torchlight the hand is floating*—where the bison is being shaped—*quickening now*—and released, and the willowy man, with his ochre spear poised in the darkening cave—*under the mistletoe, in the ochre world, among the bats and abstracted forms*—is awakened again for the first time.

In Privacy

In privacy—*all of its channels opening like mouths.*
In privacy—*lilies blooming, guerilla fighters leaping through
    shattered windows.*
In the hot springs, on the mountainside, the man and woman
    kiss—a casual isolation, clear light, water, water thinking
    its single thought—but they can't keep it on the screen.
*Jets are strafing the besieged city, the man is rolling on the city's
    black floor, it is a kind of electrified dance—*
They had tossed the coin into the basket. They had placed the
    canned vegetables, soups, and fish—*The child is beyond
    hunger. He has chewed his clothing, and now he is sitting
    "patiently," now*—it seems to one watching from outside
    his body—*he has lost the way to his stomach to his skin—*
The crows curve into the draw. The sparrows are a vagueness
    in the brush.
The man is being beaten on every channel the child—
The hummingbirds keep mistaking the woman's blouse for a
    red flower, keep hovering, buzzing, looking.
The couple keep wanting to speak, keep forming sentences in
    their minds, the sentences keep changing the landscape.
    The greenness, the wavering greenness—*what they agreed
    was a greenness, what they agreed was a wavering*—keeps
    turning into trees.
Into trees, where the birds keep *perching.*
The gunshots so far away now the dangers.
The man and woman are alive, not hungry. Their privacy is
    full of voices.
They are in the hot springs, kissing, they are the moment's
    fiction, a complex of occasions, a seeing inside the seeing
    inside—
That they had bodies was the first problem, the first grace.

That they had found each other was the first accident, the
    first miracle.
That their eyes had been formed by the landscape. That they
    heard what their ears let them hear.
But the mind keeps wanting the beyond, the unravelling—
The distance between melody and improvisation is the mind's
    distance, the mind's distance but the breath, fingers, all
    the intricate organs are a calling from the actual.
The dying child is inside is tapping a stick against the actual
    there is mud in the solo there is light.
The lungs keep thinking in the dialect of breath. The fingers
    keep tapping the keys, keep—Is it surprise they crave?
    the moment arriving and arriving and arriving and
    arriving?
There are winds in the reeds, small appetites in the trees.
That they, themselves. What they are.
That the light coating the trees, the branches, bark, each
    needle shivering in, shivering *with*.
That a radiance is shaping itself, approaching them, calling
    them.
How they were formed is the first truth they keep forgetting.
    That the forgetting is part of it. That the forgetting is
    their task. Or to remember so deeply—*memory crackling
    in the bones, all the particles of memory dazzling the flesh*—
    the first facts (mud, water), the skin's love of, the skin's
    longing for—
A helicopter spills over the ridge, battering the air—there is a
    violence in the trees a rough hand stirring the branches.
    Sunglasses, and behind them, a glance, a witnessing, a
    darkness filling all the hollows.
Then a quiet rising from the earth, flowing through the trees.

There is a long passage there are shadows crossing out the
        blue flowers the steady thud of footsteps on a wooden
        deck something—the beam of a dying flashlight?—
        moving among the scrub oaks a cool breeze a lantern
        flickering through blowing branches a tin lantern the
        sound of a tin lantern rapping a tree trunk clouds
        darkening a red sunset ideas forming crows falling
        there are sentences lurking in the sagebrush—
When they feel along all of its edges
When they find the seam
When they know how easily they could slip through
When they see how red their voices are
When they feel the light pouring over the branches
When they hear the sunset rushing along the ridge top—
What will they be the breath of? Whose hunger will they
        think they are?

ABOUT THE AUTHOR

Jon Davis is a professor of creative writing at the Institute of American Indian Arts in Santa Fe, New Mexico. A graduate of the University of Montana (B.A., 1984; M.F.A., 1985), Davis has previously published three chapbooks and one full-length collection of poetry, *Dangerous Amusements* (Ontario Review Press, 1987).

ABOUT THE BOOK

Scrimmage of Appetite was designed and typeset on a Macintosh in Quark XPress by Kachergis Book Design of Pittsboro, North Carolina. The typeface, Adobe Garamond, was designed by Robert Slimbach and is based on a typeface designed by the sixteenth-century printer, publisher, and type designer Claude Garamond. Adobe Garamond was the first Adobe Originals typeface.

    Scrimmage of Appetite was printed on sixty-pound Glatfelter Supple Opaque Recycled and bound by Thomson-Shore, Inc., Dexter, Michigan.